REVISED EDITION

Unleashing the SUPERNATURAL Power of GOD *in Your Life*

10 Godly Principles to Walk in
Your Fullest Potential

BY PROPHETESS TAMMY LAWRENCE

Unleashing the SUPERNATURAL Power of GOD *in Your Life*

Revised Edition

Prophetess Tammy Lawrence

STAR STORIES PUBLISHING LLC

Published by Star Stories LLC
Revised and Expanded Edition

Paperback ISBN: 978-1-7345437-2-8
EBOOK ISBN: 978-1-7345437-3-5

Cover design by Ariel Cornwall

PRINTED IN THE UNITED STATES OF AMERICA

Dedication

I dedicate this book to all believers in Almighty God who yearn for a deeper and more intimate walk with Him. His love flows endlessly, and His power remains unshakable.

This book is especially dedicated to my mother, whose unwavering encouragement and strength have shaped me into who I am today. To my father, whose profound wisdom has enriched my life in immeasurable ways. I am truly blessed to have had both as pillars in my journey.

To my son, may you walk in this revelation, rising as the mighty man of valor you were created to be. Stand firm in the things of God, knowing that His purpose for your life far exceeds anything you can imagine.

To my daughter, may you embrace the fullness of God's plan for you, shining brightly in His grace and walking boldly in His calling. I love you both with all my heart.

Special thanks to my dear sister in Christ from Vol. 1, whose support, encouragement, and wisdom have been invaluable in my journey. You are a true life coach, and I am forever grateful for your guidance.

To all my cherished brothers and sisters in Christ, who have stood with me in prayer, labor, and unwavering faith, I thank God for each of you. May this book stir your heart, ignite a fire in your souls, and uplift you all immensely.

God bless you all, always.
Prophetess Tammy Lawrence

Contents

Dedication iv

Part One: Positioning for the Supernatural 1

Introduction 2

Chapter One: Heaven's Holy Word Power 6

Chapter Two: Praying in Tongues 17

Chapter Three: Obedience 26

Chapter Four: Faith - A Core Value 33

Chapter Five: Taking Authority 42

Chapter Six: Enter into His Presence 51

Chapter Seven: Thanksgiving 59

Part Two: Perfecting the Supernatural 63

Chapter Eight: Warfare in the Supernatural 64

Chapter Nine: Great Expectation 75

Chapter Ten: The Power of Love 81

The Conclusion: Stepping into the Supernatural 87

Part 3: Supernatural Notes 90

Notes 91

Part One
Positioning for the Supernatural

Introduction

"Now unto him that is able to do exceedingly abundantly above all that we ask or think, according to the power that worketh in us," Ephesians 3:20 (KJV)

Blessings! This book is written from a biblical standpoint. I am writing this book to share some of the keys that have been revealed to me by the Holy Spirit of God Almighty and how He wants His Chosen Vessels of Honor to obtain all that He has for us.

There is so much more to living a life of true, authentic power and happiness that has been available to the believer since the beginning of time. Unfortunately, we have not yet truly tapped into the fullness of who we really are and all that has been invested in us as the sons and daughters of the Almighty God in order to release a complete manifestation of the fullness of our capacity.

In the supernatural realm, according to the Word of God, we can obtain all that we need to help us live a successful and victorious life. There is much to be said about God's supernatural provision and the power that He has given to every single believer in Him. God desires for all of His Sons, male or female, to walk in the fullness of power and dominion in order to be established and to be fruitful.

Now there is a huge difference between the supernatural power that comes from God, the heavenly Creator, versus the demonic and/or psychic realm of occultic practices that operate in mysticism, divination, and magic. These practitioners operate from an unholy realm to bring control, manipulation, confusion, opposition, and every evil work.

Some of what they perform has been viewed as a form of the supernatural. However, know that these practices are NOT of God, the heavenly Creator of the universe. Instead, they are a copycat version that has a form of godliness but denies the very power thereof, for God Himself does not make us do anything against our own free will.

Neither does the God of the Bible condone any forms of spells, potions, or demonic dabbling of any sort. God, the heavenly Creator, opposes this type of foolishness. The Bible clearly tells us to put away all manner of evil.

Ephesians 5:11-17 (NIV) says it this way:

"Have nothing to do with the fruitless deeds of darkness, but rather expose them. For it is shameful even to mention what the disobedient do in secret. But everything exposed by the light becomes visible, for it is light that makes everything visible. This is why it is said: Wake up, O sleeper, rise from the dead, and Christ will shine on you. Be very careful, then, how you live, not as unwise but as wise, making the most of every opportunity, because the days are evil. Therefore, do not be foolish, but understand what the Lord's will is."

Hallelujah! God wants us, His Chosen, to walk in the heart of obedience and obtain all of His divine blessings, which come down from Him. We have a God-ordained right to receive all of the benefits that are available to us when we surrender our hearts and lives unto the things of Jesus Christ, the author and finisher of our faith.

Jesus is a prime example of how we can walk in the supernatural to obtain healing, deliverance, breakthrough, joy, peace, restoration, miracles, and so much more.

However, there is something that is required from each of us, which is what this book of enlightenment brings to the table and challenges all of us to achieve.

The following information contains divine secrets and strategies of Almighty God. These supernatural keys will transform your life!

As you read this book with guidance from the Holy Spirit, you will learn the techniques of prayer, praise, faith, and many more methods as you embrace your supernatural potential and walk in your ordained destiny.

Unleash the Supernatural Power of God in your life, and you will never be the same again!

As you grow in your true purpose spiritually and embrace all that God has for you, you will begin to see the manifestation of all of God's promises in your life like never before, and this manifestation will change your life forever.

Chapter One
Heaven's Holy Word Power

"For verily I say unto you, that whosoever shall say unto this mountain, Be thou removed, and be thou cast into the sea; and shall not doubt in his heart, but shall believe that those things which he saith shall come to pass; he shall have whatsoever he saith" Mark 11:23 (KJV)

Speaking the Word of God is one of the main ways through which we can release the supernatural power of God into our lives. I have personally experienced many mighty breakthroughs that have come from what I call "*Holy Word Power*". This means that when spoken aloud, the Word of God is so powerful, that it will move heaven to manifest any good thing in your life.

I am truly a living testimony of Heaven's Holy Word Power. Without operating it, I would not be here today. I have lived it and seen it at work on many occasions. I have spoken the Word of God over others that were in desolate circumstances and have watched them walk out the manifestation with breakthroughs. I love Heaven's Holy Word Power because it unleashes the power of God supernaturally. It brings a turnaround in present situations and future circumstances that would not have changed without being spoken to with the power and authority given to us by Almighty God.

Think about when God spoke everything into existence as it is written in His Holy Word. Did you know that this is how you can speak and immediately begin to see the manifestation? Yes! We, as heirs of the Kingdom of God, also have the very same authority and ability to speak the Word and then see the manifestation follow. This is clearly pointed out to us in the book of Genesis 1:1-5 (KJV):

"In the beginning, God created the heaven and the earth. And the earth was without form, and void; and darkness was upon the face of the deep. And the Spirit of God moved upon the face of the waters. And God said, Let there be light: and there was light. And God saw the light, that it was good: and God divided the light from the darkness. And God called the light Day, and the darkness He called Night. And the evening and the morning were the first day."

As you can see, God began with an empty and void situation until He began to speak to the circumstance and immediately something started happening. The text tells us in Genesis 1:3, *"God saw that it was good."* He witnessed the manifestation! Once the light came, the Bible says that He divided the darkness from the light. This also tells us that when light comes, darkness is removed, or as I say it: *"Darkness has to flee."* God used the power of light to create.

I heard this in the spirit one day as I was sitting in my room, thinking about things in my life that were not exactly the way I wanted them to be. I heard the Holy Spirit speak to me. He simply said, *"The power to create."* I was so startled and so very surprised, but when I really began to think about the meaning of those words, I started to understand what He was trying to show me. I gained insight into the vastness of God's creative power as I meditated on all of the wonderful things that He has brought into existence according to the Holy Scriptures.

Speak first, and the manifestations will follow; the greatest of which is the creation of man when God breathed into Adam of His spirit. The way God can speak with creative authority and power is the same way we can as heirs to His throne. In Luke 1:28-31, God sent Angel Gabriel unto Mary with the Word from on high about the immaculate conception of Christ. And immediately she received the Word, the manifestation came. Mary simply told Angel Gabriel, *"Be it unto me according to thy Word."*

Oh, this is so powerful because Mary recognized the Word of God and its creative power. Even though she didn't completely understand how this could happen to her in the natural sense, Mary believed and trusted in the Power of God's Holy Word. She received the Word and just as it was spoken, it surely came to pass. We can live our lives in righteousness and holiness but still have a desolate situation until we begin to use Holy Word Power. We must begin to speak life into our situations through faith and the belief that a breakthrough can happen no matter how dark the situation may seem. According to Romans 4:17 (KJV), if we have faith and walk in the ways of God we can *"call those things that be not as though they were."*

God created us in His image; He sent Jesus to redeem us and to give us power and authority to *"tread upon scorpions and serpents."* This is a great heritage of power and authority. The Word tells us that *"they shall not harm us or touch us."* Luke 10:19 (AMPC) says:

"Behold! I have given you authority and power to trample upon serpents and scorpions, and [physical and mental strength and ability] over all the power that the enemy [possesses]; and nothing shall in any way harm you."

So, we can exercise this authority by speaking to the mountains or situations in our lives to bring about change and victory. I believe that Holy Word Power releases angelic help and assistance. It also moves the Holy Spirit to rearrange things in our favor.

We can see this clearly in the book of Acts when the apostles were arrested for preaching the Gospel. God sent His angels to release and assist them in the matter. Acts 5:18-19 (NIV) reads:

"They arrested the apostles and put them into public jail, but during the night the Angel of the Lord opened the doors of the jail and brought them out."

My God, Oh Glory Hallelujah! We don't have to tolerate lack, poverty, sickness, disease, sadness, or any other types of bondage. We can be free by using Heaven's Holy Word Power today! This is how we get Heaven to move on our behalf and utilize divine intervention.

There is no reason why we should sit around and tolerate our lives being void and without form or with darkness covering the face of our deep when we can emulate our Father God and say, "Let there be light!" We can begin to call in whatever it is that we are expecting God to do in our lives. By activating the Power that the Lord has invested in us, we can create and invite His assistance to bring His favor into our lives.

I know it truly blesses God when He sees the sons and daughters of His Kingdom walking and talking just like

Him, I know because He said it Himself in John 15:7-8 (KJV), He said:

"If ye abide in me and my Word abides in you, ye shall ask what ye will, and it shall be done unto you. Herein is my Father glorified, that ye bear fruit; so, shall ye be my disciples."

I believe that all of Heaven is still waiting for the sons of God to be revealed, according to Romans 8:19, but for this to be accomplished, it will take some Holy Word Power.

To experience a transformative change in your life and unleash the power of God like never before, it is imperative to conduct a self-audit of the words you have been speaking or professing. If the words you analyze do not promote or edify the listener, I encourage you to replace them with words that bring vitality and empowerment.

I have discovered that negative speaking comes from allowing negative thoughts to enter our minds and our hearts. This is why the Word of God tells us in Philippians 4:8 (KJV):

"Finally, brethren, whatever is true, whatever is noble, whatever is right, whatever is pure, whatever is lovely, whatever is admirable, if anything is excellent, or praiseworthy, think about such things."

Our thoughts have a powerful impact on our speech, and ultimately, our destiny. Negative thoughts can lead to negative speech, which can in turn hinder our progress and even sabotage our future. Before I understood the full significance of Holy Word Power, a wise prayer warrior once cautioned me that speaking negatively can result in a crop failure of our harvest due to the power of our words.

Upon hearing this, I immediately began to pray the prayer of repentance. I applied the principle of binding and loosing, restricting all negative words, and releasing words of love, faith, and vitality into my circumstances going forward. I had to recall 2 Corinthians 10:5 (AMPC):

"*Cast down every thought and every high thing that exalted itself against the knowledge of God. Inasmuch as we refute arguments and theories and reasoning and every proud and lofty thing that sets itself up against the true knowledge of God; and we lead every thought and purpose away captive into the obedience of Christ the Messiah, the Anointed One.*"

Glory to God! During prayer, I have often found it necessary to plead the blood of Jesus over my mind, commanding it to be still and at peace. Without this practice, I have noticed that the enemy can try to infiltrate my thoughts with distractions and negative whispers. I have learned to nip these thoughts in the bud, as negativity can take root and lead to harmful speech.

To guard against this, I put on the helmet of salvation to protect my mind and thoughts, while also guarding my heart. Sometimes, negative words may escape our lips due to underlying heart issues that we may not even be consciously aware of. In this case, always remember Luke 6:45 (NIV):

"For out of the abundance of the heart the mouth speaks."

I personally believe that this is why there are so many people with heart diseases in the world today. My theory stands that because people have allowed an abundance of negative feelings to get rooted deeply into their hearts, it has become common for millions of people to have heart problems or die of heart attacks or heart diseases. The illness of the heart is one of many reasons that many are hospitalized and sick in our society today.

Our heart is one of the most vital organs in our body; it is essential to always keep it guarded and pure. We cannot allow the enemy of our souls to cause us to miss our purpose or destiny all because we are not protecting our hearts. The Bible tells us,

"Above all else, guard your heart, for everything you do flows from it" Proverbs 4:23 (NIV).

If you sincerely want to get things turned around in your life and you are serious about seeing the manifestation of the Lord's blessings released in supernatural measures, then you should do a complete heart checkup. Ask the Holy Spirit to shed light on any area of your heart that is malfunctioning and expose any root of bitterness.

Whatever is in your heart that may have caused you to utter negative words out of your mouth, simply repent and ask the Holy Spirit to remove and cleanse all things that may be hindering you from receiving His complete best from operating and flowing effortlessly. Believe me, it works! I am living proof that when we get our hearts right with God, and we make ourselves available to Him, He begins to manifest Himself like never before.

Ask God to '*create in you a clean heart and renew a right spirit in you*' as it is directed in Psalm 51:10 (NIV). I have had to do this many a day because living in the physical realm, we can get caught up in the ways of the world, and our natural man (flesh) may want to allow discord to flow in or out of our hearts.

But we must be mindful and know that *"The spirit gives life, the flesh counts for nothing"* according to John 6:63 (NIV). We also know that *"nothing good lives in me, that is, in my flesh"* Romans 7:18 (AMP). We should want to profit from the spirit and have the good fruit of the spirit at work in our lives, and not just live in mediocrity.

If we limit ourselves to relying solely on our minds, hearts, wills, or emotions to guide our actions in speech, we will never reach our full potential or rise above the norm. However, if we open ourselves up to the spirit of the living God and allow Him to take full residence in our lives, we can access the realm of excellence and greatness that we were created to operate in from the very beginning. By shifting away from old carnal ways of thinking and speaking, we can tap into God's divine status and fulfill our true potential.

This is why Holy Word Power speaking is so vitally important and needed amongst believers in this day and hour.

I once had a colleague who had a vocabulary easily comparable to a sewer. Every word he spoke was a curse word. One day, I decided to ask him a very powerful question, which I believe gave him something profound to think about. I asked him, "How can you ever expect your life to be blessed if everything that comes out of your mouth is a curse?"

He just looked at me in complete shock, but I knew it had hit home with him and positively impacted him. Shortly after, I noticed he began to change his way of speaking. I praise God for that word from the Holy Spirit that day because I know I helped him.

God gave this word to me through prayer and meditation, and when I use the Heavenly Holy Word Power key to unlock and tap into the power of the supernatural realm, miracles begin to come forth. On the other hand, when I stop, it stops. Therefore, I have learned firsthand to integrate Holy Word Power in my daily routine consistently, making it a sustainable tool in my lifestyle.

I have learned that when I walk into the places that God has designed for my life, upon entry, I watch what I say and am mindful of my speech. You will be amazed at the results that you will receive once you turn this dynamic key of Heaven's Holy Word Power.

I dare you to try it now and begin to experience God's supernatural best for your life.

Chapter Two
Praying in Tongues

"But ye, beloved, building up yourselves on your most holy faith, praying in the Holy Ghost." Jude 1:20 (KJV)

The Bible instructs us to *"pray and to pray without ceasing"*, as stated in 1 Thessalonians 5:17. It's important to remember that prayer takes many forms—whether kneeling, lying prostrate, or simply crying out before the Lord. These are just a few examples. However, I want to focus on the way the Lord has placed on my heart to share with you in this chapter.

Praying the Word of Almighty God is tremendous, especially when you need God to respond quickly to your dilemma. I have found that when you pray the Holy Scriptures word for word, with pure intentions in your heart, and direct them to your needs and situations, miracles begin to happen. In this, we tap into the supernatural realm instantly because it gets the attention of the Holy Spirit.

I know for certain that the main way we can be assured that we are praying the Word of God is by praying in the spirit, also known as "praying in tongues." This is an awesome technique that my spiritual Godmother taught me. When we apply the Word of God to every area of our lives—whether physical, financial, relational, or emotional—it unleashes a supernatural manifestation like never before. The essence of praying in tongues is to allow the Spirit of God within us to pray through us, guiding us in every circumstance.

Although "Praying in the Spirit" is a topic that has sparked much debate among various people of faith, Ephesians 6:18 instructs us to pray *"with all prayers and petitions, praying at all times in the Spirit."* Whether one believes in it or not, praying in the Spirit is a powerful tool and deadly weapon against the enemy. Unfortunately, many Christians still do not fully believe in the power-packed gifts of the Holy Spirit.

I understand that many believers and theologians have not embraced this for various reasons, such as a lack of understanding of the gift or fear due to its misrepresentation by those who have not allowed the Holy Spirit to demonstrate its true effectiveness. However, I challenge every believer of the Bible, the risen Savior, and the supernatural things of God Almighty, to tap into this heavenly gift and give it a try.

You might think it doesn't make sense. Due to improper teaching or religious constraints, you may have been led to believe it has its time and place, or that it's not for you. But let me tell you this: the devil is a liar! The enemy does not want you to have this anointed, powerful weapon because with it, you will begin to hear from God like never before. You will also gain the ability to disrupt Satan's influence over your life, your family, your community, and even your nation.

Believe me, this is a gift given to us from on high to break the spirit of opposition, and it truly works. The gift of tongues is so unique that the Bible describes, in the book of Acts, how *"when the believers were in the upper room praying in unity, they began to speak with new tongues."* These tongues moved through the Spirit and *"appeared as tongues of fire."*

This is incredibly powerful because fire consumes and destroys. When we pray in the Spirit, using our heavenly prayer language, we effectively burn up the enemy's schemes and counter his assignments against our lives. It's no surprise that the enemy of our souls wants to keep the people of God from understanding or receiving this powerful gift of praying in the Spirit. He doesn't want you to ignite the traps and devices he has set to ensnare you.

It's no coincidence that he will ultimately be cast into his eternal dwelling—the lake of fire—where he and all his demons will be utterly consumed and destroyed. That is his expected end! Believe me when I say that you need this gift now, more than ever, as a mighty man or woman of God to stop the enemy's plans against your life.

I have faced situations in my own life where I felt completely lost. Yet, as I was prompted by the Holy Spirit to pray in my heavenly prayer language, divine revelation and direction began to unfold. I didn't know what I was saying, but the Holy Spirit did, *"for He knows the mind of God,"* according to 1 Corinthians 2:11. As you follow the leading of the Holy Spirit, you'll begin to walk a clear path of divine guidance and manifestation.

That's why, once you are fully equipped with the whole armor of God, you shouldn't just pray but also pray in the Spirit. God has given us this gift to unleash supernatural power and assistance on our behalf. Even though we may not always understand what we are saying or praying, the Holy Spirit knows and understands our heavenly utterances.

The Bible says, *"The Spirit Himself makes intercession for us with groanings which cannot be uttered"* Romans 8:26

(KJV). You may not always know what to pray or how to pray something through, but the Spirit of the living God is here to assist. He knows precisely how to intercede for us, going before the Father on our behalf. We also have access to this divine assistance through our heavenly gift of tongues.

It's incredibly reassuring to know that we serve a God who understands our deepest yearnings and will never leave us helpless or hopeless. He has us covered through the precious Holy Spirit, who takes our spirit-filled prayers and presents them as groans before our Heavenly Father. I love the fact that we have been given a holy Comforter who has our back.

The Word of the Lord assures us that when we don't know what to say or how to pray, *"the Spirit will teach us the words to say,"* according to Luke 12:12 (NIV). It is truly awesome that we serve a God who is our helper, comforter, protector, deliverer, and so much more!

When we pray in the Spirit, we access the heavenly realms, which bring us answers, clarity, guidance, and divine angelic assistance. Heaven begins to move as we release our faith through these prayers, building up not just our faith but our *"most holy faith"* Jude 1:20 (KJV). This is especially crucial when our faith is challenged, and doubt or disbelief starts to creep in.

Extended periods of praying in tongues are a practice that saints throughout the ages have practiced and have led to profound breakthroughs—and I have witnessed it firsthand. If you seek more spiritual power, pray more in the Holy Spirit!

Praying in our holy prayer language brings divine release. While regular prayer may take time to press through, praying in the Spirit often works in a more effective and timely manner. There is something about Holy Spirit-filled prayer that transcends natural understanding.

As the Bible states, *"The things of the Spirit are foolishness to those who are not spiritually discerning"* 1 Corinthians 2:14 (NIV). The natural mind may struggle to grasp how this spiritual truth operates, but regardless of personal feelings, I speak from both actual truth and personal experience. Praying in the Spirit can cause significant turnarounds, break chains, and send the enemy fleeing in defeat.

We need not remain in bondage to doubts about our spiritual prayer language any longer. The Holy Spirit comes to bring liberty, freedom, and truth. This may be difficult to understand for those who do not have a close relationship with the Holy Spirit, the one who comes alongside to help and comfort us. This experience is as real as it gets.

I can relate to those who question or feel skeptical about it because I once thought, "Those people speaking like that must be crazy; it doesn't take all of that!" I remember my own skepticism. But one day, I watched a Christian program that discussed the baptism of the Holy Spirit with the evidence of speaking in tongues, and I felt a strong desire to learn more.

I believe God had me right there listening to that program because He knew I was curious and needed to know more. I had heard about it in church and from other Christians who operated in this gift, but I didn't fully grasp its reality or importance.

Then, my perspective completely shifted one night after attending a Bible study. My pastor spoke on the topic of the Holy Spirit—something I had never heard him address before. At the end of the service, he issued an invitation that changed my life forever.

It was a powerful moment. I cried like a baby as the Spirit took over me—I couldn't control it, and it was neither fake nor conjured. A bright light enveloped me, accompanied by an overwhelming sense of peace, power, and grace all at once.

I got into my car, utterly amazed, unable to believe what had just happened. Despite being a Christian and attending church for many years, I had never fully grasped the significance of the spiritual gift of speaking in our heavenly prayer language.

When the Holy Spirit touched me and ignited a passion for His glory, and when I received the baptism of the Holy Spirit, it was a profound and transformative experience—like a new birth. I felt a deep change within my entire being, and God revealed a new aspect of Himself to me that I had never known or understood before. I felt completely transformed, and this experience has been a part of my life ever since.

What I love most about this gift is that it's available to all the saints of God. It's remarkable how we can accept and appreciate that people from different cultures around the world speak in their own languages, yet struggle to understand that heaven, too, has its own unique language.

How limited of a perspective it is to presume that the divine realm should conform to our human ways of communication. The heavenly language is unlike any of our earthly languages. There is a different way of speaking in the heavenly realm and an entirely different way of reasoning and perceiving things. How can we be so short-sighted and believe that we have it all figured out? God is a great big God, and we can't confine Him to our limited understanding. No matter how much we think we've got Him figured out, He never ceases to amaze me!

The Bible says, *"For my thoughts are not your thoughts, neither are your ways my ways, declares the LORD."* Isaiah 55:8 (NIV)

I am so glad that I embraced this spiritual truth because it has truly been a blessing to my life. You must remember, it's only for the asking. If you receive a gift in the mail with your name on it, you have two choices: you can either accept it or return it, but the choice is yours. Regardless of your decision, just know that it's available.

When received, the gift of speaking in tongues can be activated, providing benefits and a power source, offering new facets of divine revelation that you would not be able to access otherwise.

Here is a powerful prayer key for igniting your supernatural flame through speaking in tongues:

I pray that if you have not yet experienced or received the anointed gift of speaking in the Holy Spirit's heavenly language of tongues, you will seek God for divine revelation, and as this revelation unfolds, may the fire of the Holy Ghost ignite a flame in your heart, soul, and spirit that can never be extinguished, in Jesus' mighty name. Amen!

Chapter Three
Obedience

"If ye be willing and obedient, ye shall eat the good of the land; but if ye refuse and rebel, ye shall be devoured with the sword" Isaiah 1:19-20 (KJV)

Obedience is the main key that unlocks God's supernatural power and authority in your life. There are many examples in the Word where we see the power of God move once His chosen begin to obey the Word of the Lord. The Bible states, *"If you are willing and obedient, you shall eat the good of the land"* Isaiah 1:19 (NKJV). This reminds us that we must first be willing, meaning we must desire to do what is right. We must make a conscious decision, out of our God-given free will, to lead a Godly life in righteousness and faith.

God is deeply concerned with the condition of our hearts and our willingness to follow His commands, for *"the Spirit searches all things, yes, the deep things of God"* 1 Corinthians 2:10 (NKJV). From the very beginning with Adam and Eve, disobedience led to humanity's fall from kingdom dominion. Their failure was a test of obedience to God. He wanted to see if they could continue to use the "key of obedience" to walk in the supernatural realm, where their spoken words, thoughts, or decrees would immediately manifest.

This is how creation was designed to operate, and it reflects the way God intended us to live since the dawn of time. But once Adam and Eve allowed the enemy to ensnare them and disobeyed God, they lost their divine, supernatural kingdom dominion. The Word of God tells us that *"obedience is better than sacrifice"* 1 Samuel 15:22 (NKJV), so there is nothing we can offer to God that holds more value than our obedience. When we exercise this mighty power of obedience in our lives, we open the door to supernatural manifestations on a whole new level.

I'm reminded of the time when God told Abraham to take his son, Isaac, and offer him as a sacrifice. This request must have completely stunned Abraham. Naturally, he didn't want to sacrifice the son he had waited so long to have. But in an incredible act of obedience, despite the heartache, Abraham set out on the journey, determined to obey the Word of the Lord. Once God saw Abraham's unwavering obedience and trust, He provided a ram in the bush for the sacrifice, releasing Isaac back to his father. Abraham's blessing was a direct result of his act of obedience according to Genesis 22:1-12 (NKJV).

Similarly, we see Queen Esther save an entire nation by obeying the Word of the Lord through her uncle Mordecai. Esther's courage and obedience changed the course and destiny of her people. She went against the laws of the kingdom, risking her own life to do what was right. In Esther 4:16 (NKJV), she boldly declared, *"Go, gather together all the Jews who are in Susa, and fast for me. Do not eat or drink for three days, night or day. I and my attendants will fast as you do. When this is done, I will go to the king, even though it is against the law. And if I perish, I perish."*

Queen Esther's decision to approach the king could have led to her death, but she knew in her heart she had to obey God's voice, regardless of the cost. Imagine if she hadn't been brave enough or if she had chosen to disobey—an entire nation could have been lost. Yet, her obedience led to deliverance for her people.

In my own life, as I have chosen to walk in obedience to God's will and calling, I've experienced supernatural power and favor. I've come to realize that the Bible is the manual God has given us for guidance and clear decision-making. It is the road map that leads directly to victory and the blessed life if followed correctly. In Deuteronomy 28:1-14 (KJV), the Word tells us:

"And it shall come to pass, if thou shalt hearken diligently unto the voice of the Lord thy God, to observe and to do all his commandments which I command thee this day, that the Lord thy God will set thee on high above all nations of the earth. And all these blessings shall come on thee, and overtake thee, if thou shalt hearken unto the voice of the Lord thy God."

Oh, praise the Lord, hallelujah! Who wouldn't want God to elevate them and have His blessings overtake them? I know I love to see God bless His people, and I certainly enjoy walking in His blessings myself. Don't you? But here's the thing—there's a condition. The Word says *"if"*. That *"if"* means everything is contingent on us doing what God has commanded. If we obey, all the promised blessings will come. If we do not, they won't.

To receive those overtaking blessings, we must do what the text says: *"Hearken!"* To hearken means to take heed, pay close attention, listen carefully, and be all ears. Isn't that truly amazing? God is urging us to listen closely, pay attention, and follow His commands because we could be deceived if we fail to hearken. I just love the Lord God! He leaves nothing out. His Word presents us with choices—He gives us free will to choose right or wrong, but He also graciously points us in the right direction and tells us the best way to choose.

In the second half of Deuteronomy 28, the Word warns us about the consequences of disobedience. There are countless examples throughout the Bible of how many of God's chosen people—kings, prophets, and leaders—disobeyed the Lord, causing their destinies to be delayed. Plagues, curses, and even death were released as a result. Disobeying God is entirely too risky, and the consequences are severe. Proverbs 16:25 (KJV) reminds us: *"There is a way that seemeth right unto a man, but the end thereof are the ways of death."*

God desires for us to trust Him enough to obey His Word and not walk in our own ways. He knows the path we should take and what is best for us in every aspect of our lives. I thank God for His love and desire to bless us, which is so evident throughout the Bible. He gives us the opportunity to make the right decision through our free will, allowing us to choose His best. But this requires something from us, and that something is obedience.

As I reflected on the word *obedience*, I began to see its connection to the heart, and I felt a sense of surrender. This is what it's all about—surrendering our will to the will of Almighty God. Only then can we become pliable and moldable in His hands. Think about the potter who has a lump of clay in his hands; he can mold and shape that clay into a brilliant masterpiece because it is pliable.

In the same way, God wants to shape and reshape us until we are walking and talking like Him. But this requires a willingness to be pliable, which can only come through complete obedience to His will and His Word. Many may say, "Well, I don't know the will of God for my life." But I tell you: it's simple. As you begin to obey His Word, you will start to walk in His will. Think of it this way—His Word *is* His will, and His will *is* His Word.

As you hearken and obey, His divine purpose for your life will supernaturally unfold. You'll find yourself walking right into your destiny. Just try it, and you'll see it for yourself. You'll be well on your way to accomplishing all that God has truly ordained for you. Being a doer of the Word of God, and not a hearer only—"*But be ye doers of the word, and not hearers only, deceiving your own selves*" James 1:22 (KJV)—will unlock the power to walk in the supernatural manifestation of God's promises.

Without turning this key of obedience, you may never truly reach your fullest potential or fulfill your purpose. If you search within yourself and realize that you're not fulfilling your destiny—knowing that you have so much to give and live for—and you feel something must change for things to improve, trust me: the way to turn things around is to leave behind the old ways and simply tell God, *Yes!*

That one word—Yes—to God Almighty is the catalyst that will launch you like a rocket into your supernatural destiny. You'll experience favor, blessings, and miracles like never before. To embrace the will of God is to embrace His supernatural power and provision for your life. This is only accomplished when you surrender your will by turning the key of obedience.

Chapter Four
Faith - A Core Value

"Now faith is the substance of things hoped for, the evidence of things not seen." Hebrews 11:1 (KJV)

When we walk by faith in God and believe what He says about our identity in His Word, we begin to see blessings unfold in our lives. This is truly remarkable because God is a God who unleashes the supernatural and desires to see His sons and daughters living a blessed life full of His favor.

One day, as I was reading the Word of God, I came across the verse that said, *"If you do not stand firm in your faith, you will not stand at all."* Isaiah 7:9 (NIV). I believe the Spirit of the Living God was personally letting me know that I was about to walk through some challenging times that would test my faith. It was going to require me to stand firm in my belief.

At the time, I had been dealing with very pressing situations, making serious, life-changing decisions. Trust me, it was not an easy time for me. But God was trying to let me know that I had to have faith, knowing that He would see me through as I walked with Him, allowing Him to guide my steps and lead me out of one of the most trying times of my life.

Though the enemy of my soul was raging on every side, I knew that I could win the battle for my destiny by having great faith. After all, the Apostle Paul tells us in 1 Timothy 6:12 (NIV), *"Fight the good fight of the faith,"* because the main battle we face in this life, especially as believers in God, is the battle for our faith.

The enemy knows that if he can tear down your belief system and get your confessions misaligned, causing you to speak negatively, he can come against you, your dreams, and even your destiny. This is why, *"without faith, it is impossible to please God"* Hebrews 11:6 (NIV). God is a God who moves by the Spirit of faith. The entire chapter of Hebrews is dedicated to faith, emphasizing its essential role in receiving anything from the Lord.

During those trying times, I had to stand firm and hold on to God, and this truth still holds strong today. The faith battle is ongoing as you grow through different levels of your life in your walk with God, but if you know what I know, you can win! You can come out victorious!

That's why the Apostle Paul writes, *"I have fought the good fight, I have finished the race, I have kept the faith"* 2 Timothy 4:7 (NIV). My God! We need to understand why the Apostle wrote this the way he did. He recognized the importance of faith and was teaching us that without it, we cannot effectively complete our assignments in life.

Faith is what moves mountains—whether those mountains are roadblocks, obstacles, hindrances, or anything that stands in the way of achieving our goals, dreams, or heart's desires. Remember Matthew 17:20 (KJV), which reminds us that *"even faith as small as a mustard seed—the smallest of all the seeds—can move mountains."* If such a small amount of faith has the power to move mountains, just imagine the incredible things you can accomplish with great faith.

When you stand firm in your faith, believing that what God has promised will surely come to pass, you are operating at a powerful level of faith, and in doing so, you are guaranteed to receive your reward.

The Word teaches us that *"we overcome by the blood of the Lamb and the word of our testimony"* Revelation 12:11 (KJV). This is the very battle we face daily—our testimony. The enemy despises your testimony because it is the foundation of your faith and gives all glory to God. Simply by standing and proclaiming that God Almighty has healed, delivered, and set you free, you stir up the enemy's desire to silence you.

But you must know that greater is He that is within you than he that is in the world 1 John 4:4 (KJV). *"You are more than a conqueror"* Romans 8:37 (KJV), and *"you can do all things through Christ who strengthens you"* Philippians 4:13 (KJV).

I can tell you this, when I began to increase and deepen my faith walk with God, allowing Him to take full control of my life, it wasn't until then that I began to experience the supernatural in ways I had never imagined. Sure, I knew that the supernatural realm existed and that it was available for all of God's chosen people. However, I couldn't fully tap into it until I became open and available, releasing my faith in His promises for my life.

The things of God are real, and the power of God is real. When we allow God to truly show up and show out in our lives, we begin to walk and operate in our divine purpose. The supernatural realm, with all its power and wonder, is obtainable by faith. The Bible tells us there is an unseen realm, a realm that can only be accessed by faith. When we tap into this realm, we unlock the greatness our heavenly Father has designed for our lives.

It's so important to remember that without faith in God and His Word, we risk stifling the power, favor, blessings, and all the other powerful gifts and principles that God wants us to operate in. Faith is the key that releases the flow of these divine gifts into our lives.

The very first step in accessing this divine realm is placing our trust and belief in God. As the Word says, *"But without faith it is impossible to please Him: for he that cometh to God must believe that He is God and that He is a rewarder of them that diligently seek Him" Hebrews* 11:6 (KJV). This means that to approach God and develop a relationship with Him, we must first believe in His existence and understand that He blesses those who earnestly pursue Him.

If we believe that God is real—and He is undoubtedly real—then we must learn to trust Him by faith in every area of our lives. We need to be confident that He will lead us and guide us in the direction we should go.

Now, trust me when I say that there will be times when it's not easy to walk by faith or to reassure yourself that everything will be okay. However, know this: if you submit whatever comes your way to God, the author and finisher of your faith, He will see you through. This is something you can always count on.

There may be times when you feel as though you're walking with a blindfold over your eyes, unable to see your next step. But that's when God will take your hand, leading and guiding you through each moment. He delights in us when we fully yield ourselves to Him, allowing Him to demonstrate His might and power in our lives.

The Word provides many powerful examples of how simple acts of faith can bring about the miraculous. Take, for instance, the woman with the issue of blood. She had exhausted all her resources, yet when she heard that Jesus was passing by, she became desperate for a miracle. She had grown tired of being sick and tired and knew that she had to take bold action to change her circumstances.

In faith, she pressed through the crowd, determined to reach Jesus. Often, we are crowded in our minds by tradition and worldly thoughts, surrounded by negative voices and lies from the enemy. He tells us that we must remain in our current situation and that we can't reach our destiny because we lack a degree, a job, or enough money. But the devil is a liar. Just like that woman, we must rise above the odds.

The Bible tells us that she spoke to herself, declaring, "If I can but touch the hem of His garment, I KNOW that I will be made whole."

In those days, it was unacceptable for someone deemed unclean to touch those considered clean. But the real question is, were they truly clean? Were their hearts, thoughts, and actions pure? Were they walking in love and faith? The answer is no. However, this woman's faith was unlike any other.

She pressed through the crowd with unwavering determination, and when she touched Jesus, her faith was so powerful that it compelled His healing power to flow out of Him, instantly healing her. Jesus turned to her and declared, *"Your faith has healed you."* Luke 8:43-47 (NIV)

In our own lives, sometimes we must press through the obstacles of negativity, opposition, strife, confusion, sickness, and any other barriers that stand between us and the Master. Achieving a breakthrough may require us to separate ourselves for a time, immerse ourselves in the Word, fast and pray, or even cry out to God with urgency and persistence. In these moments, it's our faith that draws the healing and power we so desperately need to receive a breakthrough.

I want to reassure you, from the depths of my heart, that God will always come through for you, just as He has for me, time and time again.

Look back at the story of the Israelites when they wandered in the desert. God provided for them in a miraculous way. He sent down manna—bread from heaven—to sustain them in their time of need. This manna was no ordinary bread. It was a divine provision, given to them daily, exactly what they needed for that day.

And when some tried to hoard it, to keep it for the next day, it spoiled and became infested with maggots. Why? Because God wanted them to trust Him every single day. He was teaching them to rely on His provision and to believe that He would show up when they needed Him most.

Just as God was faithful to them, He will be faithful to you. He will provide for you in ways you cannot even imagine. I know this because I've experienced it myself. God has tested my faith, time and time again, but He has always been there, faithful and on time.

I am so very thankful that I serve a God who is true to all of His promises. I speak this from my heart, from what I know to be true, not from what I've heard or read or by any other means. I am a living testimony of His goodness and His faithfulness.

Be grateful that we serve a God who keeps His promises and a God you can always rely on. He will never leave you; He will never forsake you, and He will provide everything you need.

Trust in Him, and you will see His glory manifest in your life. You will experience firsthand what it means to *"taste and see that the Lord is good"* Psalm 34:8 (NIV)! Trust in Him and unlock the door to God's limitless provision and miraculous breakthrough through the power of Faith!

Chapter Five
Taking Authority

"Behold! I have given you authority and power to trample upon serpents and scorpions, and [physical and mental strength and ability] over all the power that the enemy [possesses]; and nothing shall in any way harm you." Luke 10:19 (AMPC)

Authority! Heavenly authority, holy authority, and spiritual authority have been entrusted to us by Jesus Christ. He is our heavenly King and great High Priest, in whom all power and authority belong. Through Him, this authority has been extended to the heirs of salvation. If you have declared Jesus as Lord over your life, then this same power and authority belong to you!

This divine authority is not just a concept but a living reality—a gift that equips us to overcome every challenge and snare of the enemy. It is the power to rise above obstacles, dismantle strongholds, and walk boldly in the victory Christ has secured for us. We have been given the divine power to stand against anything that seeks to test or challenge us. Walking in our heavenly authority enables us to witness the supernatural power of the Holy Ghost moving on our behalf.

To release this supernatural power in your life, you must truly know who you are and whose you are in the spirit. This understanding is foundational—it grounds you in the truth of God's Word and strengthens you to stand firm when the enemy comes with his schemes and attacks.

The Word of God is your weapon, your shield, and your guide. Just as Jesus stood firm during His time of testing in the wilderness, He spoke with authority and clarity, directly quoting the Word of God to the devil. *"It is written,"* He declared, countering every temptation with truth and power from the Spirit realm.

Jesus didn't engage with the enemy from the natural mind or fleshly perspective or the outer court of human reasoning—but from the spirit, where the authority of God reigns supreme. This is the same authority you have been given. When you stand on the Word, the enemy must take notice. The Spirit realm recognizes and respects the authority that comes through faith in the living Word of God.

When the enemy comes at us with attacks on our character, our family, our marriage, our ministry, our health, our finances—when he dares to touch our destiny, our purpose, or even our very lives—we must rise up in the authority of the Word of God and declare His promises boldly!

Let me tell you something: it is not about what man says, and it is not about what the world tries to dictate. It is about what the *Word of the living God* says about you. Only the Word of God holds the power and authority that the enemy respects. Nothing else can send him fleeing.

Don't you know we are living in a time where evil is rampant, and darkness tries to overshadow the light? But God didn't leave us defenseless! He gave us an instruction in Ephesians 6:11 (AMP):

"Put on the full armor of God, so that you may be able to stand up against all the schemes and the strategies and the deceits of the devil."

Oh, you better hear me today! The armor of God is not just a suggestion; it's a divine mandate! It's your protection, your power, and your preparation to withstand the battles of this age.

So, when the enemy tries to knock you down, you stand firm! When he comes for your mind, your home, or your future, you hold your ground! Clothed in the armor of

God, armed with His Word, you are more than a conqueror through Christ who loves you.

This is why the Bible urges us in 2 Timothy 2:15 (AMP):

"Study and do your best to present yourself to God approved, a workman tested by trial who has no reason to be ashamed, accurately handling and skillfully teaching the word of truth."

You've got to know the Word for yourself! You can't rely on secondhand revelation or someone else's interpretation. You've got to dig into the scriptures and let the truth of God take root in your heart so that when the enemy comes with his lies, you can cut him down with authority and the sword of the Spirit, which is the Word of God!

Stand, not in fear but in faith, declaring boldly that you belong to the King of Kings, and His power and authority are alive within you. Hallelujah! Let the devil know that he's already a defeated foe!

You may ask, "Why do I need the armor of God?" The armor is essential because we are in a constant battle. The enemy is relentless, opposing us at every turn, trying to hinder our faith, derail our destiny, and snatch our very souls. This is why you must be fully dressed in the armor of God, prepared spiritually, and equipped to fight!

The battle is not a one-time occurrence; it is ongoing, and if you are not ready to stand firm, you risk being overtaken. But hear this: you are not powerless! Isaiah 54:17 (AMP) declares,

"No weapon that is formed against you will succeed; and every tongue that rises against you in judgment you will condemn."

The Word does not say weapons won't form—they will—but they will not prosper! Hallelujah! Weapons may come in different shapes, forms, and strategies. They may be attacks on your mind, your relationships, your finances, or your purpose. The enemy will try to stop you from fulfilling the call of God on your life, but as long as you are suited up in the Belt of Truth, the Breastplate of Righteousness, the Shoes of Peace, the Shield of Faith, the Helmet of Salvation, and the Sword of the Spirit; No weapon formed against you will be able to prosper according to the authority and power of the living Word.

We as believers have been given spiritual authority to bind, loose, and cancel demonic assignments in the mighty name of Jesus! Hallelujah! There may have been many unpleasant and damaging words spoken over you, even before you came to Christ, but now that you are walking as an heir of salvation, you have been empowered to cancel all of those negative words that were professed over your life.

You have the authority to denounce any words spoken by anyone, including yourself, and cast them down in the name of Jesus! Once you are in covenant with Christ, it's all under the blood, and you can walk in the liberty that He has provided, setting you free.

In my own life, when something from my past tries to rise up, something I know I've been delivered from, I simply plead the blood of Jesus against it. I speak over my mind and my thoughts, saying, "I cover my mind with the blood of Jesus." I declare, "Let the mind that is in Christ Jesus also be the mind that is in me."

Or if I'm facing a difficult decision and the enemy tries to bring lies or confusion, I stand firm, knowing I've already prayed and heard from God. I declare, "Let the peace that is in Christ Jesus also be the peace that is in me," and then I command peace to be still over that situation in Jesus' mighty name, amen!

I've had to bind up that spirit of negative thoughts more times than I can count, over and over again, until I broke through. How did I do it? By standing in my God-given authority and taking authority over the enemy's lies and whispers.

He's been trying to get me to doubt my position as a daughter of the Most High God, but I've learned the truth; whatever you *allow*, God allows, but whatever you *disallow*, God disallows. We don't have to let the devil steal, kill, or destroy anything from us. As long as we are walking in our heavenly kingdom authority, we can stand firm, and the enemy must flee! Glory to God!

We as believers in God Almighty have been equipped with all the spiritual tools we need to overcome the enemy of our souls— tools like the Word of God, the mighty name of Jesus, the power of the precious blood of the Lamb, the presence of the Holy Spirit, and the legions of angels at our command.

This is not something to take lightly, people of God! We do not give the enemy any room to operate, for the victory has already been secured through Jesus Christ. Our responsibility is to walk in the authority that God has given us and refuse to allow the enemy any access to our lives or our place in God.

Remember, Jesus declared it is finished in John 19:30 (AMP):

"When Jesus had received the sour wine, He said, 'It is finished!' And He bowed His head and gave up His spirit."

This signifies that the ultimate victory has already been won on our behalf. Our job now is to walk in that victory by exercising our God-given authority, ruling and reigning in the power He has granted us.

We are seated in heavenly places with Christ Ephesians 2:6 (AMP)

"And raised us up with Him and seated us with Him in the heavenly places in Christ Jesus."

Clothed in royal robes by King Jesus, the Anointed One.

When we stand firm in our faith, speaking God's Word over our lives in the face of opposition, we declare to the enemy and all his forces that we are who God says we are—more than conquerors. Romans 8:37 (NKJV)

"Yet in all these things we are more than conquerors through Him who loved us."

We are the head and not the tail. Deuteronomy 28:13 (NKJV)

"And the Lord will make you the head and not the tail; you shall be above only, and not be beneath, if you heed the commandments of the Lord your God, which I command you today, and are careful to observe them."

We are blessed and highly favored, above only and not beneath!

As we walk in the supernatural potential and position as sons and daughters of the Most High, we tap into the limitless power of God. This is how we unlock His power every time, by using the key of our Kingdom Authority! Hallelujah!

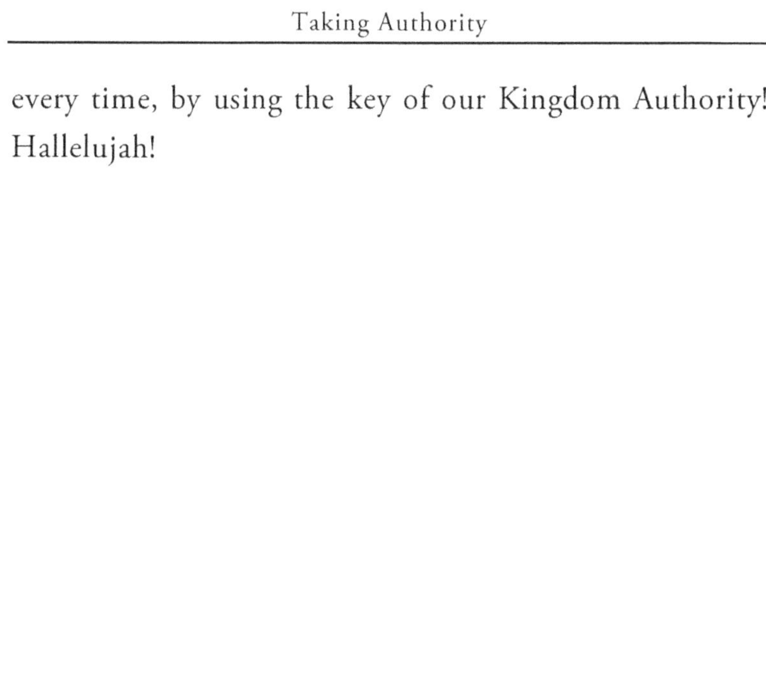

Chapter Six
Enter into His Presence

"Ask, and it shall be given you; seek, and ye shall find; knock, and it shall be opened unto you: For every one that asketh, receiveth; and he that seeketh findeth, and to him that knocketh it shall be opened." — Matthew 7:7-8 (KJV)

Praise and worship are powerful keys that activate our divine entrance into the supernatural realm. When we engage in praise and worship, we step into the very presence of the Lord, where there is fullness of joy. Psalm 16:11 (NKJV) says, *"You will show me the path of life; in Your presence is fullness of joy; at Your right hand are pleasures forevermore."*

This joy is not just an ordinary feeling; it is a supernatural strength that empowers us to tap into the Dunamis power of God. It is the explosive, miraculous force that brings about divine results. When we praise, we step into something much greater than ourselves—the very presence of God!

Praise itself is a weapon of warfare, a mighty force that can break the chains of the enemy. It releases us from the oppression of fear, heaviness, doubt, and even a broken spirit. When we lift our voices in praise and worship, we invite the very presence of God into our midst, and the atmosphere around us begins to shift.

2 Chronicles 20:22-24 (NKJV) says:

"Now when they began to sing and to praise, the Lord set ambushes against the people of Ammon, Moab, and Mount Seir, who had come against Judah; and they were defeated. For the people of Ammon and Moab stood up against the inhabitants of Mount Seir to utterly kill and destroy them; and when they had made an end of the inhabitants of Seir, they helped to destroy one another. When Judah came to a place overlooking the wilderness, they looked toward the multitude; and there were their dead bodies, fallen on the earth. No one had escaped."

The power of praise is undeniable. It not only brought victory to the Israelites, but it also brought them peace and rest. As we see here, praise precedes victory. Praise leads to breakthroughs. Praise brings rest. Just like the Israelites, we too can experience that same victory, that same peace, when we lift our hearts and voices in praise to our mighty God.

Psalm 24:9 (NKJV) declares, *"Lift up your heads, O you gates! And be lifted up, you everlasting doors! And the King of Glory shall come in."*

Praise and worship are the keys that open the gates of heaven. When we lift up our voices in praise, we invite the King of Glory into our situations. We welcome Him to intervene and bring divine help. Praise and worship bring us access to the Holy of Holies.

We should always have something to praise God for. After all, He is better than good—He is worthy of all praise, all honor, and all glory.

Isaiah 61:3 (NKJV) tells us that praise is the garment God has given us to ward off the spirit of heaviness. And when we begin to praise, the devil must flee. James 4:7 (NKJV) says, *"Therefore submit to God. Resist the devil and he will flee from you."*

Praise is our weapon to shift the atmosphere. Praise invites God's presence and brings the breakthrough we so desperately need.

But worship—oh, worship takes us even deeper. Worship is when we tell God how much we love Him, not for what He has done for us, but simply for who He is. We worship because He is God and God alone. Worship is the highest form of honor we can give to our Creator.

As Psalm 95:6 (NKJV) reminds us:

"Oh come, let us worship and bow down; let us kneel before the Lord our Maker."

There is no greater honor than to magnify, glorify, and exalt His Holy, majestic name. God deserves our worship, no matter what we're facing in life. Even when life gets hard, He is still worthy of all our praise, honor, and adoration.

When we worship God with all our hearts, I believe it touches Him so deeply that He is moved to step in and do the impossible in our lives. Psalm 22:3 (NKJV) declares, *"But You are holy, enthroned in the praises of Israel."*

Our worship invites God to move in ways we could never imagine, and it opens the door to supernatural miracles and breakthroughs. Praise and worship are not only powerful expressions of our love and gratitude toward God, but they also set the atmosphere for miracles to be released.

When we praise and worship, we invite the Holy Spirit into our lives, and when He comes, we can expect significant changes. These changes will bring forth manifested revelation, favor, and breakthrough in ways that only God can do. Praise and worship activate God's divine intervention, making the supernatural manifest in our lives.

I recall the story of Paul and Silas in prison. Acts 16:25-26 (NKJV) says:

"But at midnight Paul and Silas were praying and singing hymns to God, and the prisoners were listening to them. Suddenly there was a great earthquake, so that the foundations of the prison were shaken; and immediately all the doors were opened and everyone's chains were loosed."

Glory to God, Hallelujah! This is a powerful example of how praise and worship can shake the very foundations of any situation, loosening the chains that bind us. Whatever has you bound, whether in your mind, spirit, or life, praise and worship can break those chains and open the doors that the enemy has locked shut.

It's amazing to think that even in the darkest moments, when we feel overwhelmed, God can send a suddenly—a sudden shift that shakes up the very things trying to bind us. It is in those moments of struggle when we feel trapped or yoked in turmoil and defeat that praise and worship can bring about divine release, ushering in peace and victory.

There is nothing better than the feeling of peace, especially when you've been facing constant battles. Praise and worship are the God-given remedies that will bring us to a place of freedom and victory!

I prophetically proclaim, right now, that as you are reading this book, your enemies are defeated. As you begin to praise, your enemies are going to turn on themselves with ambushes that were set out to harm you, and instead, those ambushes will turn back on them.

Oh, hallelujah, glory to God! I pray that through the power of praise and worship, the enemy that has held up every blessing and breakthrough in your life will be utterly confused and disarmed in Jesus' mighty name.

As you begin to lift your hands and praise the God of the universe, as you begin to shout unto the Lord with a voice of triumph, as you open your mouth praising Almighty God, I decree and declare that the walls of your Jericho will begin to fall down, and you will march straight into victory! In the name of the Lord Jesus Christ, amen and amen!

There is something about praise, worship, and the lifting up of holy hands that honors our God. This act of praise also demonstrates a sign of total surrender and dependence upon a God who never fails.

I encourage you to first put on the garment of praise and allow yourself to flow into the spirit of worship, to invest in a life of praise and worship, and allow the Spirit of the living God to take you to a place in the supernatural that will change your life forever.

Psalm 100:1 (NKJV) says, *"Make a joyful shout to the Lord, all you lands!"* This joyful shout is a declaration that we are entering into His presence, and in His presence, all things are made possible. When we praise and worship, we invite God to move on our behalf, pushing us past every barrier and into the victory He has already promised us.

Psalm 34:3 (NKJV) encourages us to *"Oh, magnify the Lord with me, and let us exalt His name together."* This scripture invites us into a communal spirit of praise, lifting God up as the center of all our attention. When we come together in worship, there is a collective power that stirs up God's miraculous intervention in our lives.

Praise and worship are not just acts; they are powerful declarations that open the gates of heaven. As you enter worship, know that you are not just singing songs—you are releasing divine power that will change your life and the world around you.

Understand that praise and worship are keys to unlocking the supernatural realm, where anything is possible! Let your heart and your worship elevate, just as the Holy Spirit calls us to do. Raise your voices, make your instruments louder, and allow your praise to echo forever into the supernatural realm, for it is there that the impossible becomes possible, and God's divine presence enters into your life.

Turn this powerful key and enter the presence of the Lord supernaturally. Selah.

Chapter Seven
Thanksgiving

"And when the trumpeters and singers were joined in unison, making one sound to be heard in praising and thanking the Lord, and when they lifted up their voice with the trumpets and cymbals and other instruments for song and praised the Lord, saying, For He is good, for His mercy and loving-kindness endure forever, then the house of the Lord was filled with a cloud, So that the priests could not stand to minister because of the cloud, for the glory of the Lord filled the house of God." 2 Chronicles 5:13-14 (AMP)

Thanksgiving is a powerful element that goes hand in hand with praise and worship, yet it stands as a distinct force in the spiritual realm. It is more than just a polite acknowledgment or a routine part of our faith—it is a divine weapon!

Thanksgiving has the power to break chains, lift burdens, and open the heavens over your life. Can I tell you today that there is something supernatural about choosing to give thanks, especially when you're walking through the valley or standing in the midst of the storm? It silences the lies of the enemy, and it ushers in the presence of God.

Even in your hardest moments, choose thanksgiving, and watch God move in ways that will not only change your situation but will also transform your heart.

I remember a time when I was under heavy opposition, and everything seemed to be going wrong. I was surrounded by discouragement, feeling like there was no way out. But then, I began to reflect on all the times God had brought me through in the past, and I was reminded that the same God who delivered me before was more than able to bring me out again.

Right then and there, I made the decision to give thanks to our Father. I clapped my hands, lifted my voice, and glorified the mighty name of the Lord! I began to enter into the spirit of thanksgiving. I did exactly what the Word of God tells us to do in Psalm 95:2 (KJV). It says:

"Let us come before His presence with thanksgiving; let us make a joyful noise to Him with songs of praise!"

The Bible tells us in Psalm 100:4 (KJV) to:

"Enter into his gates with thanksgiving, and into his courts with praise: be thankful unto him, and bless his name."

Something began to shift in the atmosphere. My sadness turned into joy, my heaviness gave way to gladness, and my heart was filled with peace. I started thanking God, not just for what He had done in the past or even what He would do in my future, but for what He was doing right in the present moment.

As I declared victory over every challenge, faith began to rise, and I could feel the wind of God moving in the room. The more I gave thanks, the lighter I felt. Chains of doubt and fear were broken, and the peace of God took center stage in my heart. It was as though I could tangibly feel His faithfulness. I was reminded once again that God never fails, and most importantly, that He never will.

Think about this: when you do something kind for someone and they take the time to genuinely say, "Thank you," doesn't it make you want to help them again? It's the same with Almighty God! When we show Him that we are truly thankful for all He has done, it brings Him glory and honor and releases supernatural favor upon our lives.

A heart filled with gratitude is extremely pleasing to God. It's a spiritual posture that carries weight in the heavenly realm. The Bible is full of passages that highlight the power of thanksgiving, showing us how blessings—even miracles—can be released simply by having a thankful heart.

No matter what you're going through, or where you are in your walk with God, there is always something to thank Him for. If you can't think of anything else, thank Him for waking you up this morning and giving you another chance to experience life. Start there, and you'll find that gratitude begins to flow like a river.

Now, I declare this over you: "You are blessed and thankful, no matter what you may be going through right now in your life." I decree that "the blessings of the Lord will overtake you like never before, as you surrender to Him!"

That alone is a reason to give God thanks. Hallelujah!

There is so much power in saturating your atmosphere with thanksgiving. This is where miracles are released, burdens are lifted, and the supernatural realm becomes accessible. Thanksgiving is not just a response to what God has done—it's a key that unlocks divine favor, peace, and joy.

I urge you today to turn this key of divine power. Begin to fill your heart and your words with gratitude. Declare the goodness of the Lord and watch as His favor flows into every area of your life.

It is time to turn the supernatural key by saying it now:

Thank You, Lord!

Part Two
Perfecting the Supernatural

Chapter Eight
Warfare in the Supernatural

"[But] he who commits sin [who practices evildoing] is of the devil [takes his character from the evil one], for the devil has sinned (violated the divine law) from the beginning. The reason the Son of God was made manifest (visible) was to undo (destroy, loosen, and dissolve) the works the devil [has done]." 1 John 3:8 (AMP)

There is a war going on in the spirit realm, and the enemy is determined to stop you from stepping into the destiny and purpose that Almighty God has ordained for your life. The attacks aren't just random—they're intentional, designed to hinder the plan of God. But do not be discouraged—when God has spoken a purpose over your life, *"no weapon formed against you will prosper"* Isaiah 54:17 (KJV).

I know this to be true because I've been under attack since the very time of my conception, while I was still in my mother's womb. My mother, a mighty woman of God, has shared the story with me countless times. She endured significant trials while carrying me, spending much of her pregnancy bedridden due to complications. The situation was so severe that she was hospitalized, and my father had to sign papers acknowledging the risks, as the doctors gave little hope that either of us would survive.

The hospital even suggested bringing in a priest to pray over us before my mother went into the delivery room. My mother experienced tremendous pain and nearly hemorrhaged to death throughout the pregnancy. To add to the difficulty, I was in a breech position, and the umbilical cord was wrapped around my neck twice. By all human accounts, the odds were against us.

Many times, when you are on the brink of birthing purpose and destiny, the enemy will launch an attack. This is not just a physical battle—it's warfare in the supernatural. The enemy knows that if he can choke out or cut off your life support spiritually, he can hinder your dream from coming to fruition.

Looking back over my own life, I can see how the enemy tried to wage war against me even from birth. He aimed to stop, block, and discourage me from stepping into what God had ordained for my life. But do you know that I

John 4:4 (NIV) declares, *"Greater is He that is in you than he that is in the world."*

I am grateful that my mother is a woman of God and that she knew the spiritual battle is not fought with physical weapons but with spiritual ones. As 2 Corinthians 10:4 (NIV) states, *"The weapons we fight with are not the weapons of the world. On the contrary, they have divine power to demolish strongholds."* I believe that her unwavering faith and prayers carried us through, and by God's grace, we both survived. I entered this world safely, and my mother made it through and lived to 93 years old. *Praise God! To Him be all the glory!*

When God is moving supernaturally in your life, you can expect opposition. The enemy doesn't want you to walk into your divine calling. But the Word of God equips us to fight back. The Bible tells us in Ephesians 6:12 (NIV):

"For our struggle is not against flesh and blood, but against the rulers, against the authorities, against the powers of this dark world and against the spiritual forces of evil in the heavenly realms."

This is supernatural warfare. When you face it, you must take a stand. You have to roll up your spiritual sleeves, rebuke the enemy as Zechariah 3:2 (NIV) says:

"The Lord rebuke you!"

You don't fight on your own; the power of God fights through you. The enemy will try to make you feel powerless, but you must remember that you are anything but. The Bible declares in Romans 8:37 (NIV) that you are *"more than a conqueror through Him who loved us." And in* Isaiah 54:17 (NIV), *God promises that "no weapon formed against you shall prosper."*

Even in the midst of battle, remember the authority you carry when you stand on the Word of God. This authority is what the enemy fears. But if you're not prepared—if you don't arm yourself with Scripture—the enemy will recognize your lack of power. The Bible gives us this warning in *Acts 19:15 (AMP):*

"But the evil spirit answered them, 'I know Jesus, and I'm acquainted with Paul, but who are you?'"

This verse highlights the importance of spiritual authority. It's not enough to simply know of God; you must walk in His power and declare His Word boldly. When you do, the supernatural realm responds, chains are broken, strongholds are demolished, and victory is released.

When God is moving supernaturally in your life, the enemy will often try to initiate spiritual warfare against you, seeking to create turbulence in your mind and heart, to stir up fear and doubt, and to distract you from your destiny. But this is where you must understand that the weapons of our warfare are mighty in the supernatural realm.

When you stand firm in faith, wielding the Word of God, you activate supernatural power that breaks chains, demolishes strongholds, and releases victory in your life.

The enemy will often attempt to initiate spiritual warfare against you, stirring up fear and doubt to distract you from your destiny. But we are not defenseless. As believers, we are equipped with mighty spiritual weapons that are designed to demolish every attack the enemy tries to launch. These weapons are not of this world but are powerful in the supernatural realm.

The **Word of God** is one of the most powerful weapons we have, serving as both our shield and sword. As it says in Hebrews 4:12 (NIV):

"For the Word of God is alive and active. Sharper than any double-edged sword, it penetrates even to dividing soul and spirit, joints and marrow; it judges the thoughts and attitudes of the heart."

The Word of God penetrates deep, exposing the truth and revealing what is hidden in our hearts.

Another powerful weapon is the **Blood of Jesus**. The blood shed on the cross covers us, protecting us from the enemy's schemes and empowering us to overcome any battle. Revelation 12:11 (NIV) declares:

"They triumphed over him by the blood of the Lamb and by the word of their testimony; they did not love their lives so much as to shrink from death."

The Blood of Jesus secures our victory and brings us freedom from the enemy's grip.

Prayer is another weapon—it changes everything. James 5:16 (NIV) tells us:

"The prayer of a righteous person is powerful and effective."

When you pray, heaven moves. Prayer invites God into your situation and releases His divine intervention.

We are also equipped with the **Armor of God**. As it is written in Ephesians 6:10-11 (NIV):

"Finally, be strong in the Lord and in his mighty power. Put on the full armor of God, so that you can take your stand against the devil's schemes."

The Armor of God enables us to stand firm in the face of spiritual attacks, offering protection and power.

Another powerful weapon is **Faith**. Our faith in God is the foundation for all victory. It is by faith that we declare that we are more than conquerors through Christ Jesus.

"No, in all these things we are more than conquerors through him who loved us." Romans 8:37 (NIV)

It says that with faith, we stand assured that no matter the battle, we are victorious through Christ.

The **Name of Jesus** is also a mighty weapon in our spiritual arsenal. Philippians 2:10 (NIV) says:

"That at the name of Jesus every knee should bow, in heaven and on earth and under the earth."

The name of Jesus holds all authority, and when we speak His name, we invite the power of heaven to move in our lives.

Then there's the **prayer of agreement**, a weapon of unity and power. The Word says in *Matthew 18:19 (NIV)*:

"If two of you on earth agree about anything they ask for, it will be done for them by my Father in heaven."

When you join hands in faith with another believer, heaven responds. Agreement amplifies your prayers and accelerates your breakthrough.

Praise and worship are essential weapons in spiritual warfare. When we praise and worship, we invite God's presence into our situation and declare His greatness over all opposition. Psalm 22:3 (KJV) affirms:

"But thou art holy, O thou that inhabitest the praises of Israel."

Praise activates God's power, bringing us peace and victory. **Fasting** is another mighty weapon. Matthew 17:21 (NKJV) says:

"This kind does not go out except by prayer and fasting."

Fasting brings alignment with God, breaks chains, and releases breakthrough. When you fast, you're telling God, "I'm serious about my deliverance!"

And let's not forget the **Holy Spirit**, our guide and strength. John 14:26 (NIV) declares:

"But the Advocate, the Holy Spirit, will teach you all things and remind you of everything I have said to you."

The Holy Spirit empowers you, gives you wisdom, and strengthens you for every battle.

The **Spirit of Truth** is another weapon that exposes the enemy's lies. John 16:13 (NIV) says:

"When He, the Spirit of truth, comes, He will guide you into all truth."

Truth dismantles every deception the enemy tries to use against you.

And finally, the **Word of Testimony**—your testimony is a weapon! Revelation 12:11 (NIV) declares:

"They triumphed over him by the blood of the Lamb and by the word of their testimony."

When you testify of God's goodness, you remind the enemy and yourself of God's faithfulness.

These twelve weapons of warfare are divine tools that help us stand firm in the face of every spiritual battle. When we wield them in faith, we activate the supernatural power of God in our lives. With these weapons, we are equipped to overcome any challenge and walk in victory, knowing that with God, we are more than conquerors.

You must follow the flow of the Holy Ghost and allow Him to take total control as He promises to lead you in the way you should go and guide you with His eye. Psalm 32:8 (KJV) declares:

"I will instruct thee and teach thee in the way which thou shalt go: I will guide thee with mine eye."

He may lead you to pray a specific prayer, offer a unique praise, or engage in spiritual warfare in ways that seem unconventional—but trust His leading. When you obey, you position yourself for victory every single time.

When you dwell in the supernatural realm with God, there is no room for doubt or wavering faith. Be confident, as Philippians 1:6 (KJV) assures us:

"Being confident of this very thing, that he which hath begun a good work in you will perform it until the day of Jesus Christ."

Whatever He has promised, He will complete.

The challenges you face are designed to weaken your faith but do not give in to fear. Fear is just false evidence appearing real, and it has no place in the heart of a believer standing on the promises of God. Keep your thoughts aligned with the Word of God, for we serve a God who always causes us to triumph. 2 Corinthians 2:14 (NKJV) declares:

"Now thanks be to God who always leads us in triumph in Christ."

Remember, you are an heir to the Kingdom, empowered by the blood of Jesus, clothed in God's armor, and equipped with His Word. Plead the blood of Jesus over every circumstance, pray with boldness, and give thanks, knowing that the Messiah fights for you. Romans 8:31 (NIV) reminds us:

"If God is for us, who can be against us?"

As you walk in obedience and faith, you will see His hand move mightily in every situation. Warfare in the supernatural is not about your own strength but about surrendering fully to the power of God, who fights on your behalf.

Turn this powerful key and watch as the victory unfolds.

Chapter Nine
Great Expectation

"For I know the thoughts that I think toward you, saith the LORD, thoughts of peace, and not of evil, to give you an expected end" Jeremiah 29:11 (KJV).

When you're walking in the natural, and you're in desperate need of God to do something extraordinary in your life, you must set your expectations high! You must expect the Lord to move in ways you've never imagined in order to manifest His power and provision right when you need it most.

But there is a requirement. To see that manifestation, you need to fuel your faith. You need to stand firm with the unshakable knowing that God will deliver and that He will always be true to His Word. God is faithful and just, and His Word will never return void.

As Isaiah declares:

"So shall My Word be that goes forth from My mouth; it shall not return to Me void, but it shall accomplish what I please, and it shall prosper in the thing for which I sent it" Isaiah 55:11 (NKJV).

But it doesn't stop there. When you find a promise in God's Word that lines up with what you're believing for, that's the key! Stand on it. Declare it. Speak it into existence with unwavering faith.

The moment you speak it, the atmosphere shifts. *As Jesus Himself tells us:*

"Truly I tell you, if anyone says to this mountain, 'Go, throw yourself into the sea,' and does not doubt in their heart but believes that what they say will happen, it will be done for them" Mark 11:23 (NIV).

When you align your faith with God's promises, you are setting the stage for the miraculous. The victory is already yours! Stand on it, believe it, and see it come to pass. There is no room for doubt because God is faithful.

And when you make daily confessions, speaking His Word over your life, you will see the manifestation happen, beyond a shadow of a doubt.

In Habakkuk 2:2 (NIV), the Word of the Lord declares:

"Then the LORD replied: 'Write down the revelation and make it plain on tablets so that a herald may run with it.'"

What does this mean for us? When God speaks a promise into our lives, it is not meant to be kept in the secret places of our hearts. The revelation is meant to be written down and/or declared out loud, spoken with boldness and faith.

The Bible tells us in Psalm 45:1 (NIV):

"The tongue is the pen of a ready writer."

This means that your words and your declarations are like a pen, writing the story of your faith. And when you speak those words in alignment with God's promises, the angels take those words and run with them. When they run with God's Word, miracles begin to unfold.

I know this truth firsthand. I remember when God spoke to me and told me to buy land. He gave me a Word, a promise from Heaven. But in the natural, it didn't make sense. I didn't have the credit or the money, nor did I have the connections.

But here's the most powerful part of the story: God didn't need any of those things for His Word to come to pass. All He needed was my faith. So, I stood on His Word, and I confessed that Word every day, believing that what God had promised, He would deliver. And what did I see? I saw the manifestation of that promise far beyond what I could have ever imagined!

It wasn't because I had it all figured out. In the natural, it looked impossible. But I kept thanking God in advance, knowing that He was at work even when I couldn't see it.

And then, one day, out of nowhere, I received three phone calls—from three different people, none of whom knew each other—telling me how God had blessed them with new homes.

In that moment, I felt like God was gently reminding me to keep expecting. He was saying, "Don't stop expecting, don't stop believing, the promise is still coming, and I am still at work."

It was as if He was reaffirming to me that even when the natural circumstances seemed impossible, He was still moving behind the scenes, and His promises remained faithful.

So, I want to encourage you today—keep expecting! Keep believing! Because God is able to bring His Word to pass in your life, no matter how big or small that promise may be.

How do I know? Because with no credit, no money, and no connections, I continued to stand in unwavering faith, and just a short time after hearing the testimonies of three people who didn't even know each other, I found myself turning the key and stepping into my new home—supernaturally!

When we expect with great faith, God shows up in mighty ways!

Great expectancy is not passive. It is active faith. It is a faith that says, "I don't know how God is going to do it, but I know He will." It is a faith that says, "I will not settle for anything less than God's best for my life!"

God is a rewarder of those who diligently seek Him, as it says in Hebrews 11:6 (NKJV):

"But without faith, it is impossible to please Him, for he who comes to God must believe that He is, and that He is a rewarder of those who diligently seek Him."

No matter what you are believing God for today, whether it's healing, a breakthrough in your finances, a new home, a job, or even the salvation of your loved ones, I am here to tell you to expect it!

Whatever it is. There is no limit to what God can do. There is nothing too big or too hard for our God! (Ephesians 3:20 KJV) says:

"Now unto Him that is able to do exceedingly abundantly above all we can ask or think, according to the power that worketh in us."

God is able to do far more than you can ask, think, or imagine. His power is at work in you. There is no mountain too high, no valley too low, no situation too impossible for God to move on your behalf.

I am living proof that no matter what the situation may look like, God is faithful to His Word. Whatever He has promised, He is able to perform. And if He did it for me, He will do it for you! For God is no respecter of persons. Acts 10:34 (KJV)

If you stand in faith, if you speak His promises over your life, if you expect Him to move, He will do it.

Expect God to show up in your life. Expect Him to move in ways you've never imagined. You may not see the way, but know that God is already at work.

And when you mix great expectancy with great faith, the impossible becomes possible. God will move in mighty, supernatural ways in your life.

Great expectancy is the key that unlocks the door to miracles. It is the catalyst for God's promises to be fulfilled.

And I declare over you today that you can expect your breakthrough and expect your miracle by turning the powerful key of great expectation.

Chapter Ten
The Power of Love

"There is no fear in love. But perfect love drives out fear, because fear has to do with punishment. The one who fears is not made perfect in love. We love because He first loved us."
1 John 4:18-19 (NIV)

Love. It is the most powerful force in the universe. It has the ability to heal wounds, unite the divided, and overcome even the darkest of circumstances. Yet, love is often misunderstood, underestimated, or overshadowed by the complexities of life.

But make no mistake—true, God-given love has the power to transform hearts, renew minds, and unlock the supernatural in ways we cannot fully comprehend.

One night while in the stillness of prayer, seeking answers for the cares and concerns weighing on my soul, I heard these words clearly:

"You have to have more love in your heart."

At first, I didn't fully understand. After all, I considered myself a kind and loving person; but as I reflected on the meaning of the word "love" and thought back to past instances where I could have responded with greater grace, patience, or compassion, I realized how often I fell short.

I saw moments where frustration, pride, or an old attitude crept in, blocking the flow of love that God calls us to embody.

As the Holy Spirit ministered to me, it became clear that love isn't just a feeling or a convenient action; it's a choice, a discipline, a heart posture, and a reflection of God's character within us.

Love requires intentionality, even when faced with situations or people that challenge us. This revelation brought me to a deeper understanding of the kind of love God desires from us—a love that transforms not only our relationships but also the spiritual atmosphere around us.

It's the kind of love that stands firm in the face of adversity, that forgives when forgiveness seems impossible, and that overcomes evil with good.

1 John 4:20 (NIV) says:

"Whoever claims to love God yet hates a brother or sister is a liar. For whoever does not love their brother and sister, whom they have seen, cannot love God, whom they have not seen."

This verse challenges us to evaluate the sincerity of our love walk. How can we profess to love God, the Creator of all, if we struggle to extend love to those created in His image?

Love is not simply a feeling; it's an action and a decision. It requires forgiveness and grace, even in the most challenging situations.

The Bible calls us to a radical standard in Luke 6:27-28 (NIV), where it says:

"But to you who are listening I say: Love your enemies, do good to those who hate you, bless those who curse you, pray for those who mistreat you."

It is easy to love those who are kind to us, but it is in loving our enemies that we truly reflect the heart of God.

The Bible reminds us in 1 Peter 5:7 (NIV):

"Cast all your anxiety on him because he cares for you."

This verse teaches us to release every worry, offense, and negative emotion to God. Allowing those emotions to take root in our hearts can hinder our ability to love and can block the blessings He desires to pour out.

When love becomes the foundation of our lives, it transforms everything. It creates unity, and unity releases the power of God. Just as the Father, Son, and Holy Spirit operate in perfect agreement, so must we.

This truth is echoed in John 13:34-35 (NIV), where Jesus says:

"A new command I give you: Love one another. As I have loved you, so you must love one another. By this everyone will know that you are my disciples, if you love one another."

Love is also a purifying force. In 1 Peter 4:8 (NIV), it says:

"Above all, love each other deeply, because love covers over a multitude of sins."

When we choose to forgive and walk in love, we open the door for healing and restoration. Holding onto bitterness and unforgiveness only weighs us down, but releasing those burdens allows us to experience the freedom God intends for us.

God's love for us is the ultimate example. In John 3:16 (KJV), it says:

"For God so loved the world, that he gave his only begotten Son, that whosoever believeth in him should not perish, but have everlasting life."

This sacrificial love is the foundation of our faith. Through His love, we have redemption, grace, and the power to overcome.

The Word sums it up perfectly in 1 Corinthians 13:13 (NIV):

"And now these three remain: faith, hope, and love. But the greatest of these is love."

Love is the key to walking in the supernatural power of God. It aligns our hearts with His and unlocks the blessings He has for us. Choose love. Choose to forgive. Choose to let God's love flow through you.

When you walk in love, you are turning the key to unlock the power of Heaven's blessings and breakthroughs in your life. *"For God is love."* 1 John 4:8 (KJV) and when you choose love, you are choosing to reflect His very nature.

Love is not just a virtue; it is the gateway to the supernatural.

I declare today that God's perfect love fills your heart and soul, transforming you from the inside out. As you turn the key of His love, may it unlock the fullness of His peace, joy, and purpose in your life.

May His love bring healing to every hurt, restore every broken part, and renew your spirit with His amazing grace. As you walk in His perfect love, may it guide your every step and empower you to love others with the same compassion and understanding He has shown you.

May this perfect love cast out fear, bring restoration to relationships, and open the doors to unimaginable blessings. Know that as you turn the mighty key of the power of love, you are stepping into a supernatural realm where His power is at work in you, and all things are possible.

The Conclusion
Stepping into the Supernatural

"Do not conform any longer to the pattern of this world, but be transformed by the renewing of your mind." Romans 12:2 (NIV)

Father, I thank You for the supernatural principles that have been shared in this book. I pray that these principles have empowered every reader to walk in a deeper, more transformative relationship with You, one that will forever change the course of their lives for the better.

Lord, I pray that the key elements presented here have ignited a new passion for prayer and faith, allowing them to tap into the supernatural blessings You have made available to all believers by faith.

I thank You, Father, for opening my eyes to this truth and for entrusting me with these teachings, allowing me to experience Your fullness in my own life. You have never ceased to amaze me, and as I continue to grow in understanding, I stand in awe of Your faithfulness.

Through countless angelic visitations and supernatural experiences, You have led me step by step, teaching me how to walk with You and receive from Your mighty hand. I am so grateful, Lord, and I honor You for Your love and faithfulness.

I thank You for allowing me to share these keys that You have entrusted to me, and I ask that You continue to lead me, enabling me to share more through books and other platforms as You minister to me and as my ministry grows in You.

Lord, I pray now for every reader: I encourage them to earnestly seek You for the supernatural places You desire to take them. May they encounter more of You, Lord, as You reveal Yourself to them in greater measures. May their hearts be open to Your Spirit, and may they be led to new heights of faith and understanding.

I pray that they have been blessed by the wisdom shared in this book, and I ask that all they have learned here serve as a solid foundation for their journey into the supernatural.

May everything that You have for them, Lord, be unleashed into their lives. May You put the super on their natural as You reveal Your power and manifest in their lives in ways they never imagined.

Thank You, Father, for Your love, Your grace, and Your matchless power. May this prayer, and all that has been shared, resonate with each reader, bringing forth the fullness of Your promises in their lives.

We give You all the praise, honor, and glory, Lord. May Your supernatural power be forever unleashed in their lives.

We seal this prayer under the precious blood of Jesus Christ of Nazareth. In Jesus' mighty name, we pray. Amen!

SHALOM!

Part 3
Supernatural Notes

Notes

www.ingramcontent.com/pod-product-compliance
Lightning Source LLC
LaVergne TN
LVHW020626100826
845148LV00012B/2065

* 9 7 8 1 7 3 4 5 4 3 7 2 8 *